# The Kitty Chef

## Easy Family Recipes

Published by Tina Modugno 2016

*Dedicated to my family. To all the Moms, Dads, aunts, uncles, sisters, brothers, cousins, grandparents and family friends. May food always bring us together.*

THE KITTY CHEF: Easy Family Recipes

ISBN-13: 978-0994909367
ISBN-10: 0994909365

Copyright 2016 by Tina Modugno
Written and Illustrated by Tina Modugno
First Edition: Published November 2016

All rights reserved.
Reproduction of any part of this book for profit is forbidden.

***Illustration & Publishing inquiries: www.tinamodugno.com***
The Oreo Cat website: www.theoreocat.com

For any questions regarding the recipies contained in this book, please feel free to contact us at:
***theoreocatofficial@gmail.com***

***Disclaimer:*** *Trademarks and brands are the property of their respective owners. No claim is made to them and no endorsement by them of this book or recipes is implied or claimed.*

Part of The Oreo Cat © children's book collection

**COOKING** is something that most of us do everyday. Whether it's out of sheer need or just to have fun, it's something that is a part of our daily lives! An important part of cooking is the time that a family will spend together eating these wonderfully crafted meals! It does not have to be anything complicated, but just enough to bring the family to the table and enjoy some quality time with one another!

Quality time does not only have to be spent eating the food! It can also be spent making the food! Teaching kids about cooking and the importance surrounded by meal-time can make a positive impact on their lives! Having kids participate in the making of the food will also help give them more of an interest in eating what's in front of them! The recipes in this book are meant to do just that! This is a collection of fun and simple recipes that you can make on your own or enjoy making with someone else! These family recipes have a little of everything included so that even finicky eaters will be enticed!

In addition, we've also included some recipes especially for your cat(s)! Making treats for your pet is another great way to spend time together with your kids (as well as your pets!). It's also a great project to keep children occupied on a rainy day!

So from our family to yours, we hope that you will enjoy the little delights inside the pages of this book!

~ The Kitty Chef

***Note:*** *For video versions of all these recipes, please visit our website:* ***www.theoreocat.com***

Kiss
Cook
NipBox

# Table Of Contents

Pastas & Pizzas....................Page 5

Soups & Stews....................Page 29

Meat, Fish & Poultry....................Page 41

Vegetables & Legumes....................Page 67

For Cats & Kittens....................Page 83

Desserts....................Page 97

***Note:***
*For volume conversions on amounts and measurements please visit: www.convert-me.com*

# Pasta, Pizza and Breads

Selection
white kidney
beans
la
Molisana

# Pasta e Fagiole

***Pasta e fagiole*** or "pasta and beans" is a traditional Italian dish. Much like a soup or stew, the dish started as a peasant dish, being composed of inexpensive ingredients. While the dish varies from region to region it is most commonly made using canellini beans, Kidney beans or borlotti beans and a small variety of pasta. Preparation may be vegetarian, or contain meat or a meat-based stock. Growing up, Pasta e Fagiole was always a family favorite and was often served for entertaining large groups. This dish is also a wonderful comfort food on a cold winter's night.

### *Ingredients:*

1 liter of tomato juice
4 cups of chicken stock
2 cans of white kidney beans
3 cups of small soup pasta (we used stars)
6 spicy Italian sausages
1 tbsp of dried oregano
1 clove of garlic (minced)
2 small onions (diced)
2 tbsp of Olive Oil

### *Method:*

In a large pot, add the olive oil and brown the garlic and onions. Add the sausage and break them up with the back of a spoon or a potato masher. Cook until lightly browned. Add 1 can of beans, mix well and add the tomato juice and stock. Bring to a boil, turn down the heat and let simmer for about half an hour.

While the soup is simmering, boil the small pasta in a separate pot. Drain and set aside. Add the second can of beans to the soup and sprinkle on the oregano. Mix, turn off the heat and let the pot sit for 5 minutes. To serve, add the small pasta to a bowl and spoon on the soup over top. Serve with crusty bread and cheese.

# Creamy Rotini with Bacon & Brussel Sprouts

***Kids*** can sometimes be pretty picky when it comes to eating their veggies! Adding bacon is always a sure fire way to make something otherwise pushed aside become something utterly delicious!

### *Ingredients:*

15 - 20 fresh brussel sprouts (cut into quarters)
8 strips of fully cooked bacon (cut into bits)
2 cans (2 x 10 oz) of Chicken a la King sauce*
1 bag of Rotini pasta (454 g)
2 tbsp of butter
Fresh ground black pepper

### *Method:*

In a large pan add one tablespoon of butter and let it melt, add the bacon and brown a little. Add the brussel sprouts, stir and let brown. While veg is cooking, boil the pasta in salted water to an "al dente" state (about 5 - 7 minutes). While pasta is cooking, add the St-Hubert sauce to the pan with the brussel sprouts and bacon, mix well. Drain the pasta and add it directly to the sauce. Mix well, turn the heat to low, cover and let sit until the pasta is tender. Add the other tablespoon of butter, mix and serve with fresh ground black pepper.

Leftovers can also be eaten cold as a pasta salad!

***Note:** *If you can't find Chicken a La King sauce, you can replace this ingredient with 1 can of condensed Cream of Chicken Soup prepared to the package instructions.*

LANCIA
FUSILLI

# Beef Noodles

***Weeknights*** can often mean busy nights! Between back and forth from school or work, in addition to added homework assignments, time can end up being quite limited. This quick and easy noodle recipe is prepared in one pot and not only saves time on clean-up, but also serves up great as leftovers!

### *Ingredients:*

1.5 pounds (or 600g) of lean ground beef
3 cups of Rotini pasta
2 cups of Salad-express Vegetable Julienne
2 tbsp of butter
1/4 cup of Soy Sauce
4 cups of water
1 tsp of Sriracha sauce
1 tsp of garlic (freshly minced or dried)
Fresh Coriander or Mint

### *Method:*

In a large pan add 1tbsp butter and let it melt. Add the garlic and brown a little. Add the ground beef and mix it until it is thoroughly browned. Add the pasta and mix well. Add the water and bring everything to a boil. Turn down the heat, add the vegetable julienne to the top and cover for about 10 - 15 minutes or until pasta is al dente. Add the other tbsp of butter, mix and top with fresh coriander or mint. Serve with extra soy sauce on the side.

BELLE
Potato

# Potato Gnocchi

***Coming from*** a rather large Italian family I was lucky to be taught how to make my own pasta by hand. Although many people shy away from the subject for fear of it being too difficult, it really is not very hard at all! Potato Gnocchi is probably the simplest form of pasta making. It does not require any special skills or equipment. All it requires is a little time and some mouths to enjoy it!

***Ingredients:***

680 g / 3lb small red potatoes.
3 cups of all purpose flour (or as needed).
2 tablespoons of Olive Oil
1 tablespoon of salt
1 sprig of sage
1 cup of grated Romano cheese
2 tbsp of salted butter
Fresh ground black pepper

***Method:***

In a large pot, add the potatoes and cover them with water. Add the sprig of sage and the potatoes to a boil and let them cook until tender (about 20 - 25 minutes). Drain the potatoes under cold water and allow them to cool. To mash, you can use a potato masher, ricer or a food processor. With the skins left on, mash the potatoes and into the mash add the Romano cheese. Place the cooled mash In a large bowl or on top of a large cutting board. Slowly fold in the flour one cup at a time. Form a large ball with your dough and gently massage the ball with olive oil. Place the dough onto a dish towel and separate it into quarters. Using extra flour for dusting, and working with 1 quarter of the dough at a time, roll out the pieces into long strips about 3/4 of an inch in diameter. Cut the strips so that the slices are about 3/4 of an inch wide. Place the cut pieces on a flour dusted cookie sheet. Continue this process until all the dough is cut. Place the trays in the freezer until it's time to cook the Gnocchi. To cook, bring a large pot of salted water to a boil. Drop in the Gnocchi and when they rise to the surface they are done. Rinse, drain, mix in the butter and serve as is or with your favorite sauce!

Pep!

# Lasagna

***Lasagna*** was always one of my favorite things growing up. My Mom could always be sure to get everyone together for some quality family time whenever there was a piping hot Lasagna gracing the center of the dinner table. Gooey cheese, spicy sausage and homemade sauce made our taste-buds happy and guaranteed wide smiles and full bellies all around!

### *Ingredients:*

2 x 28 oz. cans of diced tomatoes
1 can (28 oz.) of crushed tomatoes
1 cup of white wine
1 onion (sliced)
6 celery stalks (sliced)
6 medium carrots (cut into rounds)
6 spicy Italian sausage
1 tbsp dried oregano
2 tbsp of olive oil
1 garlic clove (minced)
1 pack of fresh or dried lasagna noodles
600 grams of grated cheese

### *Method:*

In a large pot, add the olive oil, garlic, carrots, onion and celery. Stir and brown a few minutes. Add the Italian sausages and mash them with the back of a wooden spoon. Allow to brown for a few minutes along with the vegetables. Add the cans of tomatoes, wine, oregano and mix well. Bring to a boil and turn down the heat. Cover and let simmer for 1 hour. Preheat the oven to 450 degrees (F). In a large baking dish, add some of the sauce to the bottom of the dish. Cover with lasagna noodles top with sauce and cheese. Create three layers of noodles, sauce and cheese. Bake for about 40 minutes (or until the top is golden and bubbly). Cut into squares and serve with crusty Italian bread and fresh salad.

# Quick Pasta with Fondue

***Cheese Fondue*** is a Swiss, Italian, and French dish of melted cheese served in a communal pot over a chafing stand heated with a candle or spirit lamp. Like Chinese Fondue, cheese fondue is generally eaten by dipping bread, vegetables or meat into the cheese with long-stemmed forks. Although Cheese fondue has a traditional way of being served it is an ingredient that can be used in many ways! It does not only need to be used for dipping, but can also be used to create tasty dinners the whole family will enjoy!

### *Ingredients:*

1 can (28 oz.) of diced tomatoes
2 cups of elbow macaroni
2 cups of cooked cauliflower (We used frozen, just thaw before using!)
1 package (400 g) of prepared Cheese Fondue
1 bag (8 oz ) of cheese curds (or substitute for chunks of white cheddar)
3 cups of water

### *Method:*

In a large pan on medium heat, add the can tomatoes, then pasta and water. Mix and let simmer until pasta is al dente. Add cauliflower and cheese fondue and mix until fondue is melted. Add the cheese curds on top and place the pan under the broiler until bubbly.

# Stir fried chicken and noodles

***Marinated Chicken*** is not only meant for the Barbecue, but can also be used to make delightful dishes full of great flavors! Just like barbecuing, marinating the meat a few hours in advance will really help the flavors to pop! This chicken stir-fry with noodles is also a great way to stretch a small amount of chicken and be able to feed the whole family!

## *Ingredients:*

2 chicken breast (cut in cubes)
2 packages (2 x 20 g) of St-Hubert Chicken Marinade Mix*
3 onions (sliced)
1/4 cup of Olive Oil
1 tbsp of balsamic vinegar
2 cups of chicken broth
2 cups of frozen vegetables (we used broccoli and cauliflower)
1 tbsp of butter
1 bag (340 g) of broad egg noodles

## *Method:*

In a mixing bowl, add the two packages of St-Hubert Chicken marinade, Olive oil and balsamic. Mix well. Add the mix to the chicken. Mix well to cover all the pieces, cover and let sit for 1 hour in the fridge. In a large pan, add the butter and heat it. Add the sliced onions and let them brown. Add the chicken and let it brown. Add the egg noodles on top of the chicken, add the chicken broth, turn down the heat, cover and let simmer for 20 minutes. Uncover, mix well and add the frozen veg. Cook for a few minutes more or until veg is tender. Top with a little grated Asiago cheese and serve.

***Note:** If St-Hubert Chicken Marinade Mix is not available, you can use your own favorite chicken or meat marinade. Another great substitute is to use a prepared salad dressing such as "Kraft Zesty Italian" dressing.*

1934
FRESH

# Mediterranean Style Pizza

***Pizza is one of those foods*** that pleases everyone! Whether it's bought or made at home, it's always a meal that's sure to please! Making your own pizza at home is a great way to save a few dollars and you can also dress it up as simply or as complicated as you please! Whether you make your own dough or purchase a pre-made pizza crust, home crafted pizza will always be on the dinner table quicker that ordering out!

***Ingredients:***

1 prepared pizza crust
2 tbsp of Olive Oil
1 tbsp of Dijon mustard
6 slices of Italian Prosciutto
1/4 cup of pitted kalamata olives
1/2 cup of cherry tomatoes (quartered)
4 large size Bocconcini (sliced)
1 clove of garlic (shaved)
Fresh basil leaves
Salt and Pepper

***Method:***

Preheat the oven to 425 degrees (F). Combine the Olive Oil and Dijon mustard together and spread evenly over the pizza crust. Evenly place the slices of Italian Prosciutto to cover the pizza pie. Add the garlic shavings, fresh basil leaves, Kalamata olives, cherry tomatoes and bocconcini. Lightly salt and pepper and bake in the oven for 18 to 20 minutes (or until cheese is golden and bubbly). Serve with your favorite salad and potato chips.

quick
Selection
pizza
blend

# Baked Pizza Casserole

***Easy, quick and inexpensive***, this delectable Pizza Casserole recipe is guaranteed to make the whole family want to dig in!

***Ingredients:***

3 cups Bisquick

3/4 water

1 egg

2 tbsp of Greek yogurt

3 cups of spaghetti sauce (ours was homemade but you can use store bought!)

2 cups of shredded cheese (use your favorite!)

Butter for brushing

***Method:***

Preheat oven to 400 degrees (F). Grease 13x9-inch glass baking dish with butter or cooking spray. In a bowl, mix Bisquick water, egg and yogurt.

**1)** Drop dough by spoonfuls in the bottom of baking dish (dough will not completely cover bottom of dish).

**2)** Spoon half the sauce over the dough.

**3)** Cover with half the grated cheese.

Repeat steps 1-2-3. Bake for 25 - 30 minutes (or until golden brown and bubbly). Serve with your favorite side salad.

Pillsbury
Grands!
Crescent
Croissant

# Bacon, Pea and Cheese Pinwheels

***Guests dropping by*** for afternoon tea? No problem! Whip up a batch of these quick and easy crisp, buttery and warm baked pinwheels. Perfect for tea time!

***Ingredients:***

1 package (16.3 oz) of Pillsbury Grands Crescents
1/2 cup of Bacon Bits
1/2 cup of frozen peas
2 tsp of Maille Dijon mustard
3/4 cup of shredded Emmental cheese
Fresh thyme

***Method:***

Preheat over to 350 degrees (F) Carefully remove the Pillsbury Grands Crescent dough from the packaging. Using two triangles, pinch together the seam to form a rectangle. Spread on one tsp of Dijon mustard. Sprinkle on half the bacon bits, half emmental cheese and half the peas. Add a few leaves of fresh thyme. Carefully roll the dough into a cylindrical shape. Repeat these steps with the next two dough triangles. Slice each cylinder into about 3/4 inch rounds. Place slices on a baking sheet lined with parchment paper and bake for about 17 minutes (or until golden brown). Remove from oven and serve with your favorite cup of tea.

***Note:*** *You can experiment using different ingredients for this recipe! Try different cheeses, vegetables and even make a sweet version using cut up fruits or jams!*

MAPLE LEAF
Bacon
100%
Ready Crisp
7g PROTEIN PROTÉINES

# Rolled Bacon Pizza

***Crispy dough,*** warm sauce and gooey cheese are one trio that can tantalize anyone's taste-buds! Pizza is also a food that you can have fun with in the kitchen and come up with different ways of presenting it! This classic rolled pizza is great for serving as an appetizer or packing for school and work lunches!

***Ingredients:***

1 raw plain pizza dough (you can purchase an already made uncooked dough at your local grocer, or follow a pizza dough recipe of your choosing.)
1 cup of pizza sauce
2 cups of pizza cheese
12 strips of fully cooked bacon

***Method:***

Preheat the oven to 450 degrees (F) Roll out the pizza dough to form a large rectangle. Spoon on enough sauce to lightly cover the dough while leaving the edges clear. Place the bacon strips evenly over the sauce and cover with the cheese. Gently roll the dough to make a loose loaf. Don't roll it too tight or the dough will burst. Place the log on a greased baking sheet and tuck each of the ends underneath to fully close each side. Gently paint the loaf with olive oil using a pastry brush. Lightly pierce the top of the dough with holes to allow for heat to escape. Bake in the oven for 20 - 25 minutes or until golden brown. Remove from the oven, let sit for 5 minutes and slice pieces about 1 inch thick. Serve with the remaining pizza sauce for dipping.

***Note:*** *You can freeze the rolled pizzas whole. Simply thaw overnight in the refrigerator, re-heat in the oven and enjoy! In a rush? No problem! This is also great served cold!*

# Soups and Stews

# Vegetable Potage

***A great way*** to get your daily fix of veggies is in a velvety potage. Great for serving on a cold Winter's night or even served as a cold Gazpacho on a hot summer day! This vegetable potage recipe is sure to please no matter the weather!

### *Ingredients:*

1 rutabaga (cut in chunks)
1 small savoy cabbage (cut in chunks)
2 potatoes (cut in chunks)
2 cups of frozen green peas
6 - 8 cups of vegetable or chicken stock
2 tbsp of butter
1 tbsp of sesame oil
1 tbsp of ground cumin
1 tbsp of ground ginger

### *Method:*

In a large pot melt the butter and add the chunks of rutabaga, cabbage and potato, stir and brown a little. Add the cups of vegetable or chicken stock and let everything come to a boil. Add the peas, cumin and ginger. Turn down the heat, cover and let simmer for 30 minutes or until vegetables are tender. Pass through a blender or use a hand blender to cream the soup. Serve with a dollop of Greek yogurt on top and a crispy fresh baguette.

***Note:*** *This soup also freezes well! Make a large batch and freeze some for future meals. We also like to use the soup as a sauce over our favorite pasta!*

COUPE | FRESHLY CUT
SQUASH
Delicious roasted
Red Lentils
Lentejas
ground
cumin
moulu
Kiss
The Cook

# Lentil Soup

***Lentils*** are not only packed with nutrition but are also a very versatile food. With lentils, a little can go a long way! A great source of protein and fiber, these little legumes are a great asset to any kitchen pantry!

### *Ingredients:*

500 of Butternut Squash (cut in cubes)
1 cup of sliced leeks
2 cups of brown lentils
1 small sweet potato (cut in cubes)
1 small potato (cut in cubes)
2 tbsp of butter
1 tbsp of cumin
8 cups of chicken broth or vegetable broth

### *Method:*

In a large soup pot, add the butter and allow it to begin to bubble. Add the Butternut squash, leek and sweet potato and potato. Stir until the vegetables are covered with the butter. Add in the two cups of lentils. While constantly stirring, let the mixture heat for around 2 - 3 minutes. Add the cumin and mix it in well. Add the chicken or vegetable broth and bring everything to a boil. Once it begins to boil, turn down the heat, cover and let simmer for 30 - 40 minutes (or until lentils are tender). Note that we don't add salt as the chicken broth base already has salt in it. If you use an unsalted broth, you may need to add salt and pepper to taste! Serve with a fresh baguette or Naan bread.

**Note:** *May cause a few evening toots! (toot = to break wind)*

# Split Pea Soup

***Split Pea soup*** is traditionally served as a part of a French Canadian Easter meal. Along with specialties from the Sugar Shack, or "Cabanne a Sucre", Split Pea soup is a soothing accompaniment to pancakes and maple syrup, eggs, baked beans and other seasonal French Canadian goodies!

***Ingredients:***

1 tbsp of butter
2 cups of dried split peas
1 onion (cut in cubes)
4 celery stalks (sliced)
1 lb (454 g) of boneless Ham steaks (cut in cubes)
1 cup of frozen green peas
1/4 cup of White Wine
12 cups of chicken or vegetable stock
1 tbsp of parsley
1 tsp of turmeric

***Method:***

In a large pot add the butter and let it melt. Add the celery and onion and brown a little. Add the cubes of ham and mix. Add the split peas and mix well. Add the wine to de-glaze the pot. Add the 12 cups of stock, and bring to a boil. Add the frozen peas, parsley and turmeric. Turn down the heat and let simmer covered for 45 minutes. Serve with whatever sides you like!

ROMA
Piquante • Hot
SAUCISSE ITALIENNE
ITALIAN SAUSAGE
Prête à cuire • Conservée | Ready to cook • Preserved
SANS EAU AJOUTÉE
NO WATER ADDED
BOYAU NATUREL
NATURAL CASING
600g
16 AL 04
ALIMENTS QUÉBEC
CANADA

# Spicy Meatball Soup

***Quick, hearty and spicy*** this simple Meatball soup is perfect for a busy Winter night. Using Italian sausages with the casing removed to form your meatballs will leave you with a flavorful soup without needing many ingredients.

***Ingredients:***

1 tbsp of olive oil
600 g of spicy Italian sausages
1 onion (cut in cubes)
10 cups of chicken stock
Fresh thyme
1.5 cups of small soup pasta (we used stars)
2 cups of mixed frozen vegetables

***Method:***

Remove the sausage from the casing and roll out meatballs about 3/4 of an inch in diameter. Each sausage should make 4 or 5 meatballs. In a large soup pot, add the olive oil and heat. Add the onion and lightly brown. Add two cups of chicken stock and bring to a boil. Gently drop the meatballs into the boiling stock. Let cook for 5 minutes and add the rest of the stock to the pot. Add the fresh thyme sprigs (you can directly add the branches with leaves. The leaves will fall off the branches with cooking and you will be able to remove the empty branches at the end). Turn down the heat and let simmer for 20 minutes. Add the pasta and let cook for another 10 minutes. Add the frozen vegetables and let cook for 3 minutes more.

Selection
chicken · poulet

# Summer Celery Soup

***If you are the type*** of person who likes to grow lots of vegetables in the summer (or who has a father who grows them in abundance!), this summer celery soup is a great way to use up some of your favorites! The main ingredient here is celery, however you can easily add any vegetable of your preference along with it!

***Ingredients:***

1 whole Celery washed and cut into large chunks
6 carrots washed, peeled and cut into large chunks
4 onions peeled and halved
4 cloves of garlic
1 bunch of each: Chives, Parsley, Basil and Sage
3 tbsp of olive oil
12 cups of chicken or vegetable broth
Salt and pepper to taste

***Method:***

In a large pot add all your vegetables and drizzle them with olive oil. Add your stock and bring everything to a boil. Let it boil at high heat for 10 minutes and then turn the heat down and let it simmer for an hour (or until all the vegetables are tender). Let the soup cool for 10 minutes. Using a hand blender (you can also use a regular blender or food processor if you do not have a hand blender), blend the soup until it is smooth. Serve with your favorite fresh bread.

***Note:*** *This soup can also be eaten cool with a dollop of sour cream on top.*

# Meat, Fish and Poultry

education

# Ragout de Boulettes

***Ragout de Boulettes*** or Meatball stew, is a traditional French Canadian dish. It is often served during holidays or special occasions and is great for large groups. This comforting food is a great end to a rough day and will bring the taste of home to work day lunches as leftovers! There are MANY different recipe versions to make Ragout de boulettes!

## *Ingredients:*

2 pounds of ground beef or pork (or a mix of beef pork and veal)
2 onions (one finely diced and the other sliced)
2 packages (2 x 50 g) of St-Hubert Ragout Mix*
6 cups of water
6 medium potatoes
1/4 tsp of each: Nutmeg, Clove, Cinnamon
1 bay leaf
Salt and pepper

## *Method:*

Dice one onion and add it to a bowl with the ground meat. Add nutmeg, clove, cinnamon, salt and pepper and mix the meat until evenly mixed. Roll out meatballs with the diameter of around 1 inch. Set the meatballs aside. Slice the other onion. In a measuring cup add one package of St-Hubert ragout mix to 3 cups of water. Mix well. In a large pot on medium heat, brown the sliced onion in olive oil or butter. Add the pre-mixed Ragout sauce. Stir well. Bring to a bubble, turn down the heat to a simmer and add your meatballs to the pot. On top of the meatballs add 2 cups of water and the bay leaf. Cover and let simmer for 20 minutes. In the meantime, cut your potatoes into cubes. After 20 minutes, stir the meatballs and add the cubed potatoes. Let simmer for 30 - 40 minutes.

In one cup of water, add the other package of St-Hubert Ragout mix. Mix well and add to the pot. Cook for another 10 minutes to thicken and serve with pickled beats, sweet pickled onions and green peas.

***Note:** *If St-Hubert Ragout Mix is not available, you can substitute with Beef Stew Mix.*

# Chicken Cacciatore

***One Pot*** cooking is one of my favorite cooking methods. It minimizes the mess so that you can concentrate on eating rather than washing dishes!

### *Ingredients:*

4 de-boned chicken breast (680 g)
1 can (540 ml) of diccd tomatoes
2 cups of White Wine
4 celery stalks (diced or cut into chunks)
6 medium carrots (sliced into rounds)
1/4 cup of salted butter
1 tbsp of dried Oregano
Salt and pepper to taste

### *Method:*

Place the celery and carrots into the bottom of an oven safe dish. Pour in the tomatoes. Pour in the wine. Add the chicken, sprinkle with oregano, salt and pepper. Add the butter on top. Place in the oven uncovered at 475 degrees (F) for 20 minutes. After 20 minutes, turn down the heat to 375 degrees (F), cover and let simmer for 1 hour and 30 minutes. Remove from the oven, leave the cover on and let sit for 15 minutes before serving. Serve with your favorite pasta or rice.

# Roast Chicken

***Roast chicken is one*** of those recipes that is always appreciated by the whole family! Whether you're a kid, a grown up or even a cat, this is one meal that will always please everyone!

### *Ingredients:*

1 medium size whole chicken (gizzards removed)
3 carrots
3 celery stalks
1 large bunch of parsley
1/2 cup of semi-salted butter (cold from the fridge)
Fresh ground pepper

### *Method:*

Preheat the oven to 475 degrees (F). Cut the carrots and celery stalks in half and place them in the bottom of an oven-safe dish. Place the bunch of parsley into the cavity of the chicken. Place the butter under the skin on the top of the chicken between the two breasts. Sprinkle the chicken with fresh ground black pepper. Sit the chicken on top of the carrots and celery and bake in the oven for 20 minutes uncovered. After 20 minutes, turn the oven down to 350 degrees (F), cover the dish with an oven safe cover or some tin foil and let it bake in the oven for around 40 minutes (or until juices run clear when the mid-section is pierced ~ time will really depend on the size of your chicken).

Remove from the oven and let cool and serve with your favorite gravy and side dishes.

***Note:*** *The kitties can enjoy this recipe too! Just let cool, remove the skin, break up the meat and serve in a bowl with a few carrot pieces.*

Pizza Mozzarella
Cheddar • Monterey Jack
SHREDDED NATURAL CHEESE • FROMAGE NATUREL RÂPÉ
CHERRY ITALIAN
TOMATOES
BOEUF HACHÉ MI-MAIGRE
MEDIUM GROUND BEEF
BEAU BON BIEN CUIT!
MÉLANGE D'ASSAISONNEMENT POUR
TACO
SEASONING MIX
30 g

# Taco Casserole

***Anyone who loves*** Lasagna will love this yummy gooey Taco Casserole! A great week-night dinner for the whole family, this one will leave both the kids and parents asking for a second helping!

## *Ingredients:*

2 pounds of lean ground beef
2 shallots (sliced)
1 can (400 g) of whole cherry tomatoes
1 bag (334 g) of Large Size soft flour tortillas
1 package (30 g) of Taco Seasoning Mix
1/4 cup of Pickled sliced Jalapeño Peppers
1 cup of Tomatillo salsa
1 can (400 g) of refried beans
3 cups of grated cheddar cheese

## *Method:*

In a large pan, brown the shallots and the ground beef. In a bowl or a cup, mix together the can tomatoes and the Taco seasoning mix. Add the mix to the beef and shallots. Mix well and add the Jalapeños. Turn down the heat, cover and let simmer for 20 minutes. In a large baking dish, spoon some of the meat mixture onto the bottom of the dish. Cover with flour tortillas. Add more meat mixture, then add dollops of Tomatillo salsa and re-fried beans. Cover with cheese. Continue to layer this way just like you would a lasagna (We make 3 layers). Preheat the oven to 425 degrees (F) and bake for 20 - 25 minutes (or until cheese is golden and bubbly). Serve with extra salsa, sour cream and guacamole.

Selection

# Italian Style Cretons

***Cretons or Country paté*** is generally flavored with Quebec spices such as clove, cinnamon and nutmeg. Our version is a twist on the traditional dish with a switch up for a more Mediterranean style flavor.

## *Ingredients:*

500g of lean ground pork
500g of lean ground veal
1 small onion (diced)
1 tsp of dried garlic (or one fresh clove, diced)
1 tsp of black pepper
1 chicken stock cube OR 2 tbsp of Bovril (diluted into 1/4 cup of water)
1/4 cup of milk
1 slice of white bread (cut in cubes)
1/4 cup shredded Emmental or Parmesan cheese
1 tbsp Fresh thyme (removed from sprigs)

## *Method:*

In a microwave safe bowl, add the diced onion and bread cubes. Add the milk to soften the bread. Add the pork and beef and MIX WELL. Add the ground pepper, garlic and fresh thyme and mix well. Add the cheese and mix well.

**1)** Place a loose lid on top of the bowl. Cook in the microwave for 5 minutes on high heat.

**2)** Remove from the microwave and MIX WELL. Be sure to mix everything evenly.

Repeat steps two more times (for a total of 3 times in the microwave at 5 minutes). Mix well, let cool and serve with crackers or your favorite bread. Cretons can be eaten warm or cold. It is generally served on toast with yellow mustard. Store the cretons in an airtight container in the refrigerator for up to 5 days. It can also be frozen into small portions.

Arte Nova
ITALIE
Arte Nova
AUSTRALIE
SIROP D'ÉRABLE
100% PUR
BERNARD
540 ml

# Slow cooked Maple Ham

***Slow cooked ham*** is a simple recipe that yields a large amount of servings for a low cost. It's a great meal for large crowds or to conserve for weekday lunches. Here's The Kitty Chef's recipe for a slow cooked Maple Syrup ham that will make your mouth water!

***Ingredients:***

1 medium sized Rump Roast Ham - bone in and skin on. (Sized to fit your Crock-Pot)
1/4 cup of maple syrup
1 apple (cut in quarters)
1 onion (cut in half)
1 clove or garlic (diced)
1/2 cup of water
3 or 4 lemon verbena leaves

Method:

In a crock pot, place the apple quarters and the onion halves in the bottom. Remove the casing from the ham. Cut slits into the skin of the ham. With a brush, paint the ham generously with the maple syrup. Place the ham on top of the apples and onion. Sprinkle with the garlic clove and add the lemon verbena leaves. Mix whatever Maple syrup you have left with the 1/2 cup of water and pour into the bottom of the crock pot. Turn on the crock pot to high and let cook for 8 hours. Serve with rice and spoon the juice from the ham over top.

RIVAL
Crock•Pot

# Ossobuco

***Ossobuco is a traditional*** Milanese specialty of cross-cut veal shanks braised with vegetables, white wine and broth. Ossobuco can also be made using a less expensive option, Pork shank.

### *Ingredients:*

4 pork shanks
1 can (540 ml) of diced tomatoes
1 onion (cut in chunks)
4 celery stalks (cut in chunks)
6 medium carrots (cut in chunks)
2 cups of White Wine
Salt and pepper
Dried basil leaves
2 tbsp butter

### *Method:*

In a crock pot, add the celery, onion and carrot. Salt and pepper the pork shank on both sides and set them on top of the vegetables. Add the can of tomatoes over top of the shanks. Pour over the white wine. Add the 2 tbsp of butter and the dried basil. Set the crock pot to high, cover and let cook for 6 to 8 hours. Once cooked, conserve the bones as they contain marrow that is great for spreading on fresh Italian bread! Serve with your favorite kind of pasta or rice.

Company

# Roasted Sausage & Potatoes

***Weekdays at our house*** are all about easy meals. Just because it's easy does not mean it can't be tasty! Oven roasted meals are a great way to minimize time as well as cleanup and make a meal everyone will enjoy!

***Ingredients:***

6 Italian Sausage
3 shallots (cut in quarters)
2 large green peppers (cut into chunks)
1 bag (680 g) of "The Little Potato Company - Terrific Trio" potatoes* (cut in half)
3 sprigs of fresh rosemary
3 tbsp of olive oil
Salt and pepper to taste

***Method:***

Preheat the oven to 450 degrees (F). In a large baking dish, add the peppers, onions, potatoes, sausage and rosemary sprigs. Drizzle with olive oil and sprinkle with salt and pepper. Mix everything up and place in the oven for 1 hour (mixing two to three times during the hour). Remove from heat and serve with your favorite fresh bread and cheese.

***Note:** *Any small size or miniature potatoes will work for this recipe.*

AYLMER
Selection
large size · calibre gros
12 eggs oeufs
ROMA
shredded cheese blend · mélange de fromages râpés
AYLMER

# Italian Baked Eggs

***Eggs*** are a staple in our house! They can be used to make many mouth-watering recipes, but they are also a great quick-fix meal solution! Italian baked eggs is a great meal solution for a busy night!

### *Ingredients:*

6 eggs
1 can (28 oz.) of diced tomatoes with Italian spices
1.5 cups of shredded mozzarella cheese (or any Pizza cheese mix).
1 tbsp of butter
½ cup of diced Italian Coppa, ham or bacon (we used Italian Coppa).

### *Method:*

Preheat the oven to 425 degrees (F) In an oven safe dish, add the whole can of tomatoes, tbsp of butter and diced Coppa. Bake in the oven for 15 minutes. Remove from the oven and add the six eggs to the dish, cover with cheese. Put back in the oven and bake for another 10 minutes (or until cheese is bubbly). Serve with fresh Italian bread.

metro
0.550 kg
19.82
$ 10.90
FILET TRUITE ARC-EN-CIEL
FRESH RAINBOW TROUT FILLET

# Baked Rainbow Trout and Broccolini

***Trout is a tasty fish*** that makes for a quick and easy meal that you and your cat can both enjoy! This quick and simple recipe from is perfect for sharing with your feline friends!

## *Ingredients:*

2 Rainbow Trout fillets (boneless with skin removed)
8 to 10 stems of broccolini
1 bunch of fresh coriander
2 tbsp of Olive Oil
Salt and pepper to taste

## *Method:*

Preheat the oven to 425 degrees (F). On a large piece of tinfoil, add the two tablespoons of Olive Oil. Place the broccolini stems on top of the Olive Oil. Salt and pepper the Rainbow trout fillets on both sides and place on top of the broccolini. Place the coriander on top of the fish. Completely seal the foil around the fish to form a package. Place the package on a cookie sheet and bake in the oven for 20 - 25 minutes. Serve with rice.

***Note:*** *Leftovers are perfect for making cold trout salad sandwiches the next day! Just add a little chopped celery and mayo and serve on your favorite bread!*

ARTISAN SERIES
MARVINI
BASIL
BASILIC

# Italian Steamed Tilapia

***Tilapia is a great*** versatile fish. It has a tender meaty texture and a very distinct flavor. It partners great with pastas, rice and other grains. Not only is Tilapia a great food for human consumption, but it is also a great treat for your feline friends!

### *Ingredients:*

3 Tilapia fillets
1 package (400 g) of ripe vine cherry tomatoes (cut in halves)
1/2 cup of pitted Spanish olives
1/2 cup of fresh basil leaves
1 tbsp of lemon juice
1 tbsp of Olive Oil
1 tbsp of butter
Salt and pepper to taste
Feta cheese for topping

### *Method:*

Salt and pepper the Tilapia fillets on both sides and set aside. In a large pan on high heat, add the olive oil, cherry tomatoes, basil and olives. Bring to a sizzle. Add the Tilapia fillets on top, turn down the heat to a minimum, add the butter and cover the pan. Allow the Tilapia to steam until cooked through (about 20 minutes). Serve over your favorite pasta or rice. We serve it with a simple garlic butter Risotto-style pasta. Garnish with crumbled feta cheese.

TERRIFIC TRIO
Little Potato Company
St-Hubert
Sauce
POUTINE
Lafleur
PORC ET BACON - PORK & BACON

# Pork Sausage Poutine

***Poutine*** is a classic Quebec dish. It is generally made with french fried potatoes, cheese curds and slathered in brown gravy. The traditional story is that Poutine originated in the 1950's in Warwick, Quebec, at a greasy spoon restaurant. Upon being asked to add cheese curds to a customer's fries, the owner responded, "Ça va faire une maudite poutine," translation, "That's going to make a dreadful mess". As a result, this delicious "dreadful mess" became one of Quebec's most popular dishes.

## *Ingredients:*

1 bag (680 g) of The Little Potato Company "Terrific Trio" potatoes* (sliced into rounds)
1 medium onion (cut into cubes)
1 pack (375 g) Pork Sausages (cut into bits)
1 can (398 ml) of St-Hubert poutine sauce (or any dark brown gravy)
1 bag (8 oz) of cheese curds
2 tbsp of butter or margarine
1 tbsp of dried basil
Salt and pepper to taste.

## *Method:*

In a large non stick frying pan, add the butter or margarine and bring it to a bubble. Add the onion and the pork sausages. Mix and cook until the sausages begin to brown. Add the potatoes and mix well. Add the dried basil and salt and pepper. Keep the heat on medium and cover the pan. Mix well every few minutes to ensure the potatoes get browned and fully cooked. In a sauce pan, empty the poutine gravy and heat. To serve, place the potato mixture in a bowl, top with some cheese curds and pour over the poutine gravy.

***Note:** *Any small size or miniature potatoes will work for this recipe.*

# Vegetables

Red Split Lentils
Lentilles rouges cassées
Red Split Lentils
Lentilles rouges cassées

# Sautéed Kale with Pancetta and lentils

***Of all the super*** healthy greens, kale is the king! It's definitely one of the healthiest and most nutritious plant foods in existence. Loaded with all sorts of beneficial compounds (some of which have powerful medicinal properties), kale is one of those versatile greens that is not only healthy but also super tasty! From chips to stir fry's, sautés and even pizzas, this leafy green is a great dinner solution!

### *Ingredients:*

1 whole kale (washed and bases of stems removed).
1 cup of cubed pancetta (Italian bacon)
1 cup of pitted kalamata olives
1 cup of red lentils
1/2 cup of white wine
2 tbsp of Olive oil
1 tsp of hot peppers (we use the ones that are prepared in oil)
2 garlic cloves (diced)
Salt and pepper to taste
1/2 cup of water

### *Method:*

In a large pot, (on high heat) add the olive oil, hot peppers, garlic and pancetta. Gently sauté until the garlic and pancetta begin to brown. Cut up the kale leaves, add them to the pot and mix well. Add the red lentils and mix well. Add the olives, wine and water and mix again. Turn down the heat to a minimum, cover and let simmer for about 20 minutes or until the kale and lentils are tender. Serve with pasta, rice or fresh bread.

***Note:*** *This recipe is great to use as a pizza topping or to add to your favorite sandwich or burger.*

Selection
white kidney beans
540 mL | 19 fl oz

# Potato and Bacon Tagine

***For this recipe*** the rendered fat from the bacon is used to cook the other ingredients. A great way to save time here is to pre-cook the bacon and conserve the fat in a jar in the refrigerator. We will cook the whole package of bacon in the oven, conserve the fat and then freeze the bacon strips so that they are ready for use when we need them.

***Ingredients:***

1 bag (680 g) of The Little Potato Company "Terrific Trio" potatoes*
3 onions cut in chunks
10 strips of Maple bacon (bacon grease conserved)
1 can (540 ml) of White Kidney beans (rinsed and drained)
Sprigs of each fresh thyme and sage
Salt and pepper to taste
1 tbsp of Olive Oil

***Method:***

Preheat the oven to 425 degrees (F) Warm the bacon grease in a sauce pan or in the microwave until it liquifies. Add the bacon grease along with the olive oil to the empty Tagine. Keeping the potatoes whole, add them to the Tagine and mix until they are covered. Slice the bacon into thin strips. Add the bacon, onion, beans, sage and thyme to the Tagine and mix well. Lightly salt and pepper and place the cover on the Tagine. Bake in the oven for 1 hour (or until the potatoes are tender and crispy).

We like to serve this dish with sides of pickled beats, pickled vegetable salad and gherkins.

****Note:*** *Any small size or miniature potatoes will work for this recipe.*

# Baked Vegetable Casserole

***Yet another use for*** Cheese Fondue, this hearty, healthy, quick and delicious vegetable casserole is guaranteed to get even those anti-veggie family members to want to take a bite!

### *Ingredients:*

1 sweet potato (peeled and cut into cubes)
1 broccoli (cut into chunks)
1 cauliflower (cut into chunks)
1 package (400 g) of cheese fondue
250 g of uncooked bacon (cut into lardons*)
1 sprig of fresh Rosemary

### *Method:*

In a large pan, add the bacon and cook until it begins to brown. Add the sweet potato, broccoli and cauliflower. Mix well, add the sprig of Rosemary, turn down the heat, cover and let steam for 15 minutes (until the vegetables are tender but still crisp). Preheat the oven to 425 degrees (F). Transfer the vegetable mix to an oven safe baking dish. Separate the cheese fondue into clumps and spread around the vegetables. Bake in the oven for 20 minutes (or until golden and bubbly). Serve with a fresh baguette.This recipe is very versatile and can be made with any type of vegetables! Cooking time may vary depending on the veggies of your choice.

***Note:** *Lardons is a French culinary term referring to thin strips of bacon cut approximately 1/4-inch thick.*

# Sprouted Lentil Salad

***Fresh sprouted lentils*** and seeds are a great source of energy! High in protein and other essential nutrients, they really are a Super-food! Not only do they serve up great in many fresh spring dishes, but they are also easy to grow yourself at home! This recipe uses fresh sprouted lentils that we grew ourselves right in our own kitchen!

### *Ingredients:*

3 cups of fresh sprouted lentils
2 tomatoes (diced)
1 cup of fresh chopped parsley
¼ cup of fresh squeezed lemon juice
3 tbsp of Greek Olive Oil
1 tsp of Sesame Oil
½ cup of green olives
½ cup of crumbled feta cheese
Salt and pepper to taste

### *Method:*

In a large bowl, add the sprouted lentils. Add the tomatoes and parsley and mix well. Add the lemon juice, Olive Oil and Sesame Oil and mix well. Salt and pepper to taste. Cover the bowl with plastic wrap and set aside in the refrigerator for 1 hour. Before serving, add the olives and crumbled feta and mix well. Serve with Pita bread.

# Sprouting Lentils

***Making your own*** Lentil Sprouts may seem a little intimidating to some, however it is really nothing to be afraid of! Not only is it super easy, it's also a great science project for curious kids!

### *You'll need:*

**1)** A large jar for sprouting
**2)** Cheese cloth
**3)** Dried lentils
**4)** Water

### *Method:*

You'll need enough dried lentils to fill ¼ of your selected jar. Measure them out and rinse them well. Drain them and add them to the jar. Add enough water to fill ¾ of the jar. Cover the jar securely with cheese cloth and set aside in a cool shaded area for 12 hours. After 12 hours, drain and rinse the lentils and return them to the jar. Prop the jar on it's side using a bowl and keep it in a cool shaded area. Continue to rinse the lentils at least once or twice daily (to preserve the moisture in the jar). Lentils generally take about a day or two to begin sprouting. We continued the process for four days until the tips of the sprouts were green. Then we harvested. Once the lentils are ready for harvest, rinse and drain them once again. You can keep them in the sprouting jar in the fridge for about 1 week. Sprouted lentils can be eaten raw or cooked!

Photo courtesy of TreeHugger.com

BLUSHING BELLE
the Little Potato Company
MAISON ORPHÉE
FOR SALADS AND GRILLED VEGGIES
POUR LES SALADES ET LES LÉGUMES GRILLÉS

# Roasted Potato Salad

***Breakfast is probably*** my most favorite meal of the day so it's a no brainer to recreate this morning delight for dinner. Oven roasted potatoes, crispy bacon and over-easy eggs are also a great way to say goodnight and not just good-morning!

***Ingredients:***

1 bag (680 g) of The Little Potato Company "Blushing Belle" potatoes* (cut into quarters)
8 strips of cooked bacon (sliced into pieces)
1 cup of sliced leeks
3 tablespoons of olive oil
Fresh sprigs of Rosemary
4 eggs
1 tsp of butter
Freshly grated Parmesan
Salt and pepper to taste

***Dressing:***

1 tbsp Dijon mustard
1 tbsp Mayonnaise
2 tbsp of olive oil

***Method:***

Preheat the oven to 375 degrees (F). In a large oven safe dish, add the sliced leeks, potatoes, bacon, rosemary and drizzle with olive oil. Lightly salt and pepper and mix everything together. Bake in the oven for 45 minutes to 1 hour. In a mixing bowl, add the dressing ingredients, Dijon, mayonnaise and olive oil. Mix well and set aside. Remove the potatoes from the oven and set aside. In a frying pan, add the butter and let it start to bubble. Cook the eggs so that they are over-easy (you can also poach them if you prefer). To serve, add some potato mixture to each bowl and place the over-easy eggs on top. Sprinkle with fresh Parmesan cheese and drizzle over the dressing. Serve with a fresh side salad.

***Note:** *Any small size or miniature potatoes will work for this recipe.*

# Sweet & Savory Salad

***Some of my favorite*** foods to eat are the simple things. There are so many foods that can be appreciated in their raw forms with little effort required! This sweet and savory salad is definitely at the top of my list of favorites! It can be enjoyed as a side dish with grilled meats or fish, or on it's own with some fresh bread. A great lunch option for school and/or work, this dish will peak the interest of any curious co-workers!

### *Ingredients:*

Half a Cantaloupe, center pits removed and cut into chunks.
1 whole tomato cut into chunks
1/2 cup of old cheddar cut into cubes
6 to 8 slices of cured Italian Coppa
1 tbsp of salted Pumpkin seeds
3 tbsp of Olive Oil
1 bunch of each fresh Mint and Oregano (lightly diced)
The juice of half a lemon
Salt and pepper to taste

### *Method:*

In a large mixing bowl, add all of your ingredients and mix together well. You can serve immediately or allow to sit in the fridge until it's time to serve.

# For Cats and Kittens

CAT
TEA
LOOSE LEAF CATNIP
Wild Organic Blend
Your favourite feline will love our blend of wild hand-harvested and organically farmed Nepeta Cataria

# Catnip cookies

***Although there are*** lots of commercial cat treats available, it's also fun to treat your cat to some homemade goodies once in a while! Making treats for your cat is a great DIY project for rainy weekends! When using any canned fish, always make sure that it has little to no salt added and does not contain any other additives, like Soy for example. Alternately, you can also purchase a can of salmon flavor cat food and use it in this recipe.

***Ingredients:***

1 can of low sodium pink salmon in water
1 cup of quick oats (small oats or oat flower is fine too)
2 tbsp of olive oil
1 egg
1 tablespoon of loose catnip

***Method:***

Drain the salmon and add all the ingredients to a bowl. Mix well. Measure out each cookie with a teaspoon. Flatten and shape a little and place on a cookie sheet. Bake at 350 degrees for 16-18 minutes. Let cool and serve with Whiskas cat milk. Store cookies in an airtight container in the refrigerator for up to a week (or freeze them).

# Tiny Tuna Muffins

***Another fun little*** treat to cook up for your cat, these tiny tuna and cheese muffins will not only make your feline happy, but they are also a great little snack to share together!

***Ingredients:***

1 can of low sodium flaked *tuna in water
1/4 cup of all purpose flour
1/4 cup of grated cheddar cheese
1 egg
Coconut oil for brushing (or you can use a non-stick cooking spray)

***Method:***

(Makes about 10 mini muffins) Preheat the oven to 350 degrees (F). Drain the tuna and add it to a mixing bowl with the flour, cheese and egg. Mix well. Using a mini muffin tin, grease 10 of the muffin cups with coconut oil (or a non stick cooking spray). Fill the greased cups evenly with the mixture. Bake in the oven for 18 - 20 minutes. Let cool, top with your cat's favorite kitty treat and serve! These are also perfectly fine for human consumption! Just omit the kitty treat topping!

***Note:*** *The same rule of thumb as far as canned fish goes applies here. Only purchase tuna with pure ingredients (tuna and water) and no added salt or preservatives. Tuna in Olive Oil can also be a good choice as long as it is well drained and rinsed and also does not contain any other additives or salt.*

# Sautéed Broccoli

***Even though*** cats don't require fruits and vegetables to balance their nutrition, replacing high-calorie treats with something fresh from the produce section is a great snack option! Broccoli is among the few fruits and vegetables that are perfectly safe for cats to eat! So the next time you cook yourself up some broccoli, don't be afraid to share!

***Ingredients:***

A few fresh broccoli florets (thoroughly washed)

1 tbsp of Olive Oil

***Method:*** In a pan on medium heat, add the broccoli florets and drizzle in Olive Oil. Lightly sauté until the broccoli is tender. Let cool, lightly smash with a fork and serve to your cat!

***Note:*** *Cats are obligate carnivores and this means that animal protein is the only type of protein that fulfills a cat's nutritional needs. Although feeding your cat snacks and special treats every so often is acceptable, always be sure to feed them a quality commercial diet approved by your veterinarian daily.*

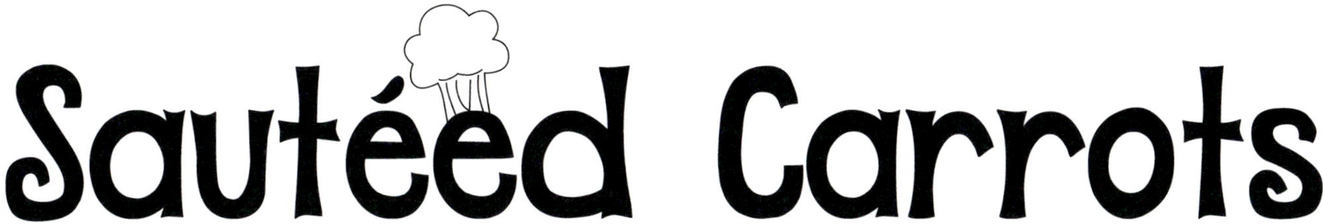

# Sautéed Carrots

***If you think*** of carrots as a treat for only rabbits, think again! Many cats love them, too. Just make sure to always offer cooked carrots, because raw vegetables can pose a choking hazard or be difficult for cats to digest.

***Ingredients:***
A handful of baby carrots (sliced into small bites)
1 tbsp of Olive Oil

***Method:*** In a pan on medium heat, add the carrot slices and drizzle in Olive Oil. Lightly sauté until the carrots are tender. Let cool, lightly smash with a fork and serve to your cat!

***Cooking Alternative:*** You can also bake the carrots whole and mash them once cooked!

***Note:***
*Foods that are toxic to cats ~ Alcohol, Chocolate, Coffee, Tea, Energy Drinks, Onions and Garlic, Nuts and seeds, Mushrooms, Rhubarb, Raw Yeast or Raw Yeast Dough.*

# Sautéed Peas

***If your dinners*** tend to include things more like green beans or peas rather than broccoli, you'll be pleased to know that these tasty greens are also a great treat for cats!

***Ingredients:***

A handful of frozen peas
1 tbsp of Olive Oil

***Method:*** In a pan on medium heat, add the peas and drizzle in Olive Oil. Lightly sauté until the peas are tender. Let cool, lightly smash with a fork and serve to your cat!

# Scrambled Eggs

***Considered by nutritionists*** to be the most perfect source of protein for animals, eggs are a great treat for humans as well as pets! They are quick, easy, versatile and perfect for sharing with your favorite furry friend!

***Ingredients:***

3 large eggs
1/4 cup of water
1 bunch of fresh parsley (chopped)
1tsp of butter

***Method:***

Crack the eggs and place them into a mixing bowl. Add the water and parsley and mix well with a fork or an egg beater. In a frying pan, add the butter and let it melt. Pour in the egg mixture and stir with a wooden spoon until the eggs cook through. Let cool and share with your cat!

metro
$ 7.13
FILET TILAPIA FRAIS CHARNU
TILAPIA FRESH FILLET MEATY

# Pan cooked Tilapia

***It's important*** to feed your cat a well balanced cat food approved by your veterinarian daily. Commercial cat foods contain important vitamins, minerals and other nutrients like Taurine, for example, that are essential to your cat's health. Occasionally feeding your cat fresh meat and fish can be a fun treat as long as they are completely cooked and fed in moderation. Always choose a cut of fish or meat that is boneless, skinless and has a low fat content.

***Ingredients:***
1 Fresh boneless / skinless Tilapia fillet
1 tsp of butter

***Method:*** In a pan, melt the butter until it bubble slightly. Add the Tilapia fillet and cook thoroughly flipping it's side half way through cooking. Let cool, mash with a fork and serve to your cat.

***Note:*** *You can use the same cooking method for other types of fish you kitty may enjoy such as cod, tuna, salmon and others. Just always make sure the fillets are boneless and skinless. Stay away from any fish that may contain very small pins (bones) such as fillet of sole.*

# Chicken Soup

***Yes! Cats can*** eat chicken soup! It is important to specify that it needs to be ***homemade*** and not store bought. The reason being that store bought may contain certain ingredients and preservatives that are toxic to cats. Onions and garlic for example are toxic. However, if you make it yourself and ensure that the ingredients are OK for your kitties… They will thoroughly enjoy it!

***Ingredients:***

1 whole chicken breast, skin on and bone in
2 celery stalks
2 or 3 carrots
1 cup of Basmati rice
10 cups of water
1 teaspoon of sugar
1 teaspoon of salt
A handful of fresh parsley

***Method:*** In a large pot, bring all of the ingredients to a boil. Let it simmer for one hour and fifteen minutes. Remove from the heat and let it cool. Let cool, remove the chicken and de-bone it. Mash the chicken meat into small pieces with your fingers, or a fork. To serve, add a bit of the chicken meat to a bowl, then add some of the broth and rice. The veggies can be pulled and used for something else if your cat is not interested in eating them. The plain broth can also be fed to young kittens using a bottle. The soup can be frozen into individual servings. Do so by freezing portions in an ice cube tray. Once the cubes are frozen pack them in a Zip-lock bag and keep in your freezer for up to six (6) months. Just heat to lukewarm and serve.

# Desserts

WIDER Mouth Jar
Dole
Peaches
Fruit Juice

# Peach Tea Cake

***Bisquick is not*** only for making pancakes! It can be used for many different deserts and is an ingredient we always keep on hand in our house! Along with canned fruits, Bisquick can help you to whip up a quick and easy desert for sharing with unexpected guests!

### *Ingredients:*

2 cups of Bisquick
1 (24.5 oz) can of Dole Sliced Yellow Cling Peaches In Light Syrup
1 egg
1 tbsp of Greek yogurt
1 tbsp of cinnamon
Butter for brushing

### *Method:*

In a mixing bowl add the Bisquick, peaches (with the juice or syrup from the can), egg, yogurt and cinnamon. Mix well. Preheat oven to 400 degrees (F) and bake for about 20 minutes (or until top is golden and a knife inserted comes out clean). Remove from the oven and brush the top lightly with butter. Let cool for 10 minutes and enjoy with a dollop of yogurt on top.

Pie Crusts
Croûtes à tarte
Chipits
SKOR
toffee bits
pépites de caramel
The Cook

# Home-style Apple Caramel Pie

***My favourite dessert*** is a thick slice of just-baked apple pie still warm from the oven. I'm always careful to save a thick wedge because apple pie is at its best the next morning for breakfast!

### *Ingredients:*

1 package of Pillsbury Pie Crusts
12 McIntosh Apples (washed and sliced with skins on)
1/4 cup of butter
1/4 cup of Skor bar bits

### *Method:*

Preheat the oven to 420 degrees (F). Line the bottom of a large pie plate with one roll of Pillsbury Pie dough. Fill the pie plate with the sliced apples. Dollop the butter over the apple slices. Sprinkle over the Skor bar bits. Cut the second pie crust into strips and place them crosswise over the top of the pie plate. Bake in the oven for 20 - 25 minutes or until the crust is golden and the apples are cooked but still tender. Serve with Vanilla ice cream or whipped cream.

quick
100% whole grain oats
rapide
Selection
bartlett
pear halves
in light syrup
Selection
pêches tranchées
à noyau adhérent

# Peach and Pear Crisp

***Crumbly fruit crisps*** are one of those staple desserts that remind us all of home. Whether you're a kid or an adult this delectable dish will make you feel like you are at Grandma's house!

### *Ingredients:*

1 large can (28 oz can) of sliced peaches
1 large can (28 oz can) of sliced pears
3 cups of quick oats
1 cup of loosely packed brown sugar
3/4 cup of semi-salted butter. Slightly cool so it can be cut into cubes. (It may sound like a lot of butter, but it's a rather large recipe!)

### *Method:*

Preheat the oven to 420 degrees (F). In a mixing bowl add the quick oats and brown sugar and mix well. Mix in the cubed butter with a pastry cutter (if you don't have a pastry cutter you can use a potato masher or a fork). Mix until the mixture becomes crumbly. Line the bottom of a baking dish with some of the crumble mixture. Drain the can peaches (conserve the juice or syrup) and add the peaches over the layer of crumble. Add another layer of crumble. Drain the can pears (conserve the juice or syrup) and add them over second the layer of crumble. Finally, top everything with the remaining crumble. Bake in the oven for about 25 minutes or until slightly golden. Let cool and serve with ice cream and spoon over some of the conserved syrup from the cans.

# Pets de Soeurs

***Les Pets de Sœurs***, or in English "Nun's Farts" are a Quebec dessert similar to a pinwheel but with an intriguing name! It is not clear as to where the name comes from, however there are theories that it relates to Quebec's love/hate relationship with the Catholic Church. The Roman Catholic church was extremely powerful in the early days of Quebec's history, and thus, squashing the rights of villagers and townsfolk. One way for the settlers to rebel against this "supreme executive power" was to make many a Catholic term a swear word. As a result, many of Quebec's profane swear words are based upon Catholic church references! Hence, out of all this was born a sweet delectable dessert with a controversial name!

***Ingredients:***

1 roll of Pillsbury Pie dough (Or you can use homemade pie dough)
1/2 cup Melted semi-salted butter.
1/2 cup of brown sugar
About a dozen whole pecans.

***Method:***

Preheat the oven to 325 degrees (F). Unroll the pie dough and set it on a flat surface. With a pastry brush, brush the dough on one side thoroughly with some of the melted butter. Sprinkle a good amount of brown sugar over the dough covering it to the edge. Gently roll the dough into a cylindrical shape. Use a bit of butter to close the end of the dough. Cut disks about 1 inch thick and gently place them on a cookie sheet lined with parchment paper. Gently bend down the upper edges of each pastry to form a shape reminiscent of a flower. Spoon over a teaspoon of melted butter over each pastry. Place a pecan in the middle of each pastry and sprinkle with additional brown sugar. Bake in the oven for 15 minutes (Or until lightly golden). Remove from the oven and let cool. The brown sugar will have melted and created a candy like texture around each pastry. You can lift this from the parchment paper and place it on top of each Pets de Sœur.
Enjoy with a tall glass of milk.

CARAMILK
DANONE
ACTIVIA
0%

# Caramilk Muffins

***Who does not like*** a mix of gooey caramel and chocolate?! These quick and easy Caramilk Muffins are sure to satisfy any sweet tooth while allowing you plenty of time to savor every bite!

***Ingredients:***

2 cups of Bisquick
1 cup of water
2 tbsp of Vanilla yogurt
4 Caramilk bars (broken into cubes)
1 egg

***Method:***

Preheat the oven to 420 degrees (F). In a large mixing bowl, add the Bisquick, egg, yogurt and water. Mix well. Add the Caramilk cubes and Mix again. Grease a large muffin tin (12 muffins) or use muffin cups. Evenly fill each muffin cup with the Caramilk mixture. Bake in the oven for 18 - 20 minutes or until golden brown. Serve with a tall glass of milk!

# Happy Blueberry cake

***Need a little something*** for the Monday blues? This blueberry lemon tea cake is a perfect treat to help turn that frown upside-down!

### *Ingredients:*

2 and a half cups Bisquick
The juice of 1 lemon (and the rind, grated)
1/4 cup of Splenda
1/4 cup of Greek yogurt
1 egg
3/4 cup of water
1 pack of fresh blueberries

### *Topping:*

Butter for brushing
2 tsp of slpenda
Juice of 1/2 lemon
Fresh blueberries

### *Method:*

In a mixing bowl add the Bisquick, Splenda, lemon juice, water, yogurt and egg. Mix well. In a spring form pan, line the bottom and the sides with parchment paper. Add some lemon zest to the bottom of the pan, then add the blueberries. Pour the batter mix on top of the blueberries. Bake in a 400 (F) degree oven for around 20 minutes (or until top is golden and a knife inserted comes out clean). Remove from oven and brush the top of the cake with butter. Let cool for 10 minutes and remove from the pan. Carefully remove parchment paper from the bottom of the cake. Mix together 2 tsp of splenda and the juice from half a lemon. Evenly pour over the top of the cake. Top with fresh blueberries for serving. Great with a side of ice cream or a dollop of creme fraiche.

MADE WITH NATURAL WHEAT BRAN, THE #1 FIBRE
TO PROMOTE YOUR DIGESTIVE RHYTHM
Kellogg's
All-Bran
Buds
BEST BEF
AVANT

# Molasses Cookies

***There is something special*** about freshly baked cookies. Whether it's the smell in the kitchen while they are bubbling away in the oven or the warm gooey goodness when you take that first bite! Cookies are definitely something that every kid and grown up alike love to come home to!

### *Ingredients:*

2 cups of All purpose flour
1 cup of All-Bran buds
1/3 cup of softened butter
3/4 cup of water
1/3 cup of Fancy Molasses
2 eggs

### *Method:*

Preheat the oven to 325 degrees (F). In a mixing bowl, add the flour, All-Bran buds, molasses, eggs, water and butter and mix until smooth. Grease a baking tray and using a tablespoon make each cookie with 2 spoonfuls of the mixture (Make six to a pan as they will be pretty large when cooked!). Bake in the oven for 18-20 minutes (or until a toothpick inserted in the center comes out clean). Makes about two trays of 6 cookies.

***Note:*** *These cookies are great for making homemade ice cream sandwiches! Just add your favorite ice cream in between two cookies and serve!*

# Raspberry muffins

***Fresh seasonal raspberries*** are among some of my husband's favorite berries for snacking on! Sometimes we wind up with more than he can eat in the refrigerator! Instead of freezing them, I like to whip up a batch of raspberry muffins! These tasty little delights are great to pop in your bag for breakfast or a quick snack!

***Ingredients:***

2 cups of Bisquick
1 small package of fresh raspberries
2 tbsp of plain Greek yogurt
2 eggs
1/3 cup of water

***Method:***

In a mixing bowl add the Bisquick, eggs and yogurt. Mix and add the water slowly. Mix again. The texture should be quite lumpy (like a scone batter). Add the raspberries (You can use whatever berries you like actually!) and mix lightly as to not break the berries too much. Grease a 12x muffin tin (or use baking papers). Add some of the mixture into each muffin cup. Preheat the oven to 450 degrees (F) and bake for 15 - 18 minutes (or until tops are slightly golden).

In Loving Memory of

# *Lucy Modugno*

# Chambalote

***My grandmother*** loved to cook, as most grandmothers do! Among her famous family recipes is a cake she called "Chambalote". With similar ingredients to an Italian Pannettone but more hearty and buttery, this cake was always on the dessert table as part of any Holiday meal. Not only did we like to enjoy this cake for dessert or a snack at tea time, we would also indulge in a slice toasted under the broiler and lightly buttered for breakfast!

### *Ingredients:*

8 eggs (extra large)
1 cup of sugar
1 cup of milk
1 tsp of vanilla
3 1/2 cups of flour
4 tbsp of baking powder
1/4 pound of butter (melted)
1/4 pound of Golden Crisco (melted)
1 cup of raisins
1 cup of chopped almonds

### *Method:*

Preheat oven to 350 degrees (F). Melt butter and Crisco together and set aside. In a Mix Master, add eggs and sugar and mix until fluffy. Slowly add milk and vanilla. Add the butter and Crisco. Mix the flour and baking powder together and slowly add to the mixer. Almonds and raisins should be added by hand. Add batter to a buttered sponge cake pan. Bake for 1 hour and 15 minutes.

Photo Credits: Emily Modugno

# *Tina and Oreo*

***Tina Modugno***, is a children's illustrator from Quebec, Canada. She has illustrated many books as well as authored and published some of her very own titles. Tina is very passionate about her work and offers a variety of services for first time authors looking to publish their own books. With experience in a variety of drawing styles, Tina works closely with authors to ensure that the highest quality standards are met. An avid animal lover, she lives with her loving husband and four cats!

***Oreo*** is a fluffy black and white kitty with quite a quirky personality! Very tiny, frail and ill, Oreo was abandoned as a young kitten by his birth mother. Rescued from a life on the street and after coming close to death, Oreo was adopted by Tina and her husband. Oreo earned his name from his coloring reminiscent of an Oreo cookie! An expert in the subject of "cat logic", Oreo has become widely known on the internet as a result of his antics.

Oreo and his owner Tina support a wonderful cause called ***The Paw Project*** and continue to strive to help teach parents and children about why cats need claws! Believe me, there are many wonderful reasons! Claws are needed for *protection,* for *exercise,* for *balance* and so much more! Can you think of some good reasons?

To learn more about Oreo visit: ***www.theoreocat.com***

***ABOUT THE PAW PROJECT***

***The Paw Project***'s mission is to educate the public about the painful and crippling effects of feline declawing, to promote animal welfare through the abolition of the practice of declaw surgery, and to rehabilitate cats that have been declawed.

For more information, visit ***The Paw Project*** website: ***www.pawproject.org***

Made in United States
Troutdale, OR
08/30/2024

22466916R00074